CW00522004

– THE –
CHARABANC

THE EARLY DAYS OF MOTORISED COACH TRAVEL

ALF TOWNSEND

AMBERLEY

First published 2013

Amberley Publishing
The Hill, Stroud
Gloucestershire, GL5 4EP

www.amberley-books.com

Copyright © Alf Townsend 2013

The right of Alf Townsend to be identified as the Author
of this work has been asserted in accordance with the
Copyrights, Designs and Patents Act 1988.

All rights reserved. No part of this book may be reprinted
or reproduced or utilised in any form or by any electronic,
mechanical or other means, now known or hereafter invented,
including photocopying and recording, or in any information
storage or retrieval system, without the permission in writing
from the Publishers.

British Library Cataloguing in Publication Data.
A catalogue record for this book is available from the British Library.

ISBN 978 1 4456 0548 7

Typeset in 10pt on 12pt Sabon.
Typesetting and Origination by Amberley Publishing.
Printed in the UK.

CONTENTS

INTRODUCTION

As a long-serving London cabbie of some fifty years, a published author of six books, and as a well-known trade journalist with many hundreds of articles under my belt, I have always held a passion for the London taxi trade and its iconic vehicle. What other profession can boast of a history stretching back to Oliver Cromwell in 1654 – over 350 years ago? He really was our founding father when he put his Ordinance before Parliament entitled, 'For ye Betterment of ye London Hackney Coach-Men' and many of his ground rules laid down are still written in the Hackney Carriage Laws up to the present day.

Subsequently, four out of my six published titles are connected to London taxis either directly or indirectly.

But my other passion for as far back as I can remember was my fascination for the charabanc, and the fact that I became a 'chara' driver in the late fifties stoked up my fascination even more – but more of that in a later chapter! The advent of the charabanc to the working classes – especially those slaving in the cotton mills in the North – seemed to evoke a special kind of freedom that not many had ever experienced before. They could save their pennies every week with their local working men's clubs and join all their mates on a lovely day out at Blackpool or Scarborough and escape the drudgery – but in those days it was always 'men only'. The workers didn't get paid for any holidays, so a day out in a 'chara' was all they got. It wasn't until the late sixties and early seventies, when the UK economy started picking up, that the workers got paid for 'Wakes Week'. That in itself spelt the inevitable death-knell for the popular charabanc, because now the workers were able to book a whole week away at the seaside B&Bs – or at one of the many holiday camps springing up all over the coasts – and now the train took the strain!

As for us 'soft' southerners, well we held on to the charabancs for a longer period. They were very popular for a day out at the races, or a 'jolly-up' with all your mates from the local pub down to dear old 'Sarfend-on-Sea'! I can well remember all the many charabanc trips I made as a youngster to places like Brighton, Margate and Ramsgate, Clacton-on-Sea and dear old Southend. My young eyes were fascinated by the sight of all the charabancs, lined up side by side in the massive parking lots alongside the Kursaal, because every single charabanc had its own distinctive colour. There was a myriad of colours, reds and blues, greens and yellows, blacks and greys and two-tones as well. Every individual company had its own livery and many were called by their colour as in 'Orange coaches', 'Black and White's', 'Blues', or 'Grey-Green's'.

But the Transport Act of 1947 started to curtail the choice of different-coloured 'charas' and the Transport Act of 1968 finally nationalised the whole industry, with Victoria Coach Station in London as its main terminus. And, apart from some independent companies who still run their 'charas' for popular fun days out, the rest of us have to contend with the clone-like and boring white coaches of National Express – ugh!

Some may call it progress, but not we 'disciples' of the old 'charas'!

ACKNOWLEDGEMENTS

My thanks to Helen and Mike Pursey, the co-editors of the South West Buses and Coaches website, for kindly supplying the vast majority of the wonderful colour images for this book – such kind and generous people. You can contact them at their website – Buses@swwg.org.uk. My thanks also to John Palmer of Broadstone Dorset, who kindly offered the five lovely old open-topped charabanc images of the people of Wirksworth, Derby.

Christopher Leach of Stafford, who runs his own website, also took time to send me some great colour images of Grey-Green coaches – plus others, so a big thank you to Christopher as well.

Last, but by no means least, my heartfelt thanks to Viv and Vernon Smith, who run the Whitby Steam Bus & Charabanc Company in Whitby, Yorkshire. They have a busy life with their daily tours around the beautiful Whitby Bay and kindly supplied me with the five wonderful colour images of their steam charabanc 'Elizabeth', and 'Charlotte', the other charabanc. Elizabeth is a bit of a 'star', because not only has she appeared in a Harry Potter film and on TV, she stole the show at last year's Lord Mayor's Parade. I think the jacket cover of Elizabeth blowing her steam tanks in Whitby Bay is a great shot and almost brings Elizabeth to life! Incidentally, it took Viv and Vern *twelve* days to steam down to London because the old girl can't do too many miles in a day! In my book that's either sheer dedication – or very shrewd marketing!

1

'CHARAS' IN THE BEGINNING

Just hearing the word 'charabanc' gives me a buzz at the thought of its long history and the joy it brought to many of the downtrodden working classes of the past. The word itself comes from the French '*char-à-bancs*', introduced in 1840s France, which means a long wagon with benches. It was later improved as a four-wheeled carriage with several forward-facing benches and was pulled by six horses – very popular with the wealthy French aristocrats and landowners to convey their guests on excursions to shooting parties and the races. The groom was seated at the rear – in a slightly lower position – of course, because, after all, he is *only* a groom! His seat would normally be above the slatted cover of the luggage compartment. The charabancs became very popular in France and when Louis Philippe of France gave one to Queen Victoria as a gift in 1844, the interest in the charabancs went big time when it crossed the English Channel!

The first thing we Brits did with the arrival of the charabancs to our shores was to drop the 'S' at the end and simply call it 'a charabanc'. And we Brits didn't need six horses to pull it, just four – or even two big English horses would do the trick! After a short while the charabanc was adapted and modified for public transport use and was entered from the rear, with five or more rows of forward-facing seats. They were modified even more a few years later after they became extremely popular for works and school outings, with even more seats being put in. But in all honesty, they weren't a very comfortable ride. They were noisy and very bumpy and the seat upholstery was very hard on the backside!

But the charabanc became an instant hit among the many thousands of workers in the mill towns of Lancashire and Yorkshire. These deprived and hard-working employees in the mills never had any holidays at all. In the bad old days when there were no holidays – or holiday pay – their only opportunity for a day out was the annual works outing to Blackpool or Scarborough. In some cases a few of the more generous mill owners would pay, or make a donation to the annual outing, but more often than not it would be the workers themselves who paid for their day out. The local working men's clubs would sometimes pay for the 'chara' out of the subscriptions from its many members. As for the individuals, they would religiously pay in a few pennies every week to the events organiser, who would enter the sum into his dog-eared notebook. Then came the big day when all the subscribers would be handed their hard-earned savings – sometimes as much as one pound or more. This sum doesn't sound like much in today's money, but if you reckon on a pint of beer being just a few pence and a packet of fags not much more, then this sum would add up to a jolly day out. In fact as the 'chara' outings became even more popular and even noisier with the excessive booze, so the complaints started to come in. But can you blame these people for letting their hair down? They had sweated for long hours in those mills having to breathe in all the floating cotton particles that caused serious respiratory diseases, and now that they were at the seaside they were determined to make the most of it.

At the very start of the horse-drawn charabanc popularity there was no shelter from the elements; the ladies would all sit in their finery and simply put up an umbrella if the sky opened up. Later on a tarpaulin-type cover was fitted and, if the heavens suddenly opened, it was deemed fitting that the men on board all gave a hand in pulling the heavy cover the length of the charabanc. There were windows of a kind on board, normally made of mica, a layer of thin, quartz-like stone that was reasonably effective. But what fascinates me is the cunning way the hauliers adapted their fleet to accommodate the busy summer season with the charabancs. Each lorry had an alternative body: a charabanc body for the summer season and a working-truck body to attach in the winter to make the vehicle viable for the whole year! But this system was simply a short-term fix, because these charabancs never lasted long; they had a high centre of gravity and were top-heavy and quite dangerous when loaded – or often overloaded. Some of the steep hills and winding roads in villages leading to popular resorts led to a number of fatal accidents which contributed to their final demise. Probably the last old charabanc notice can still be seen by Wookey Hole in Somerset, warning of the dangers to charabancs approaching the steep hill by the village of Easton. With the advent of public transport in the 1920s, many of the 'charas' were replaced with motor buses.

With the First World War on the horizon, things were starting to change in the world of the charabancs and new innovations were being displayed at the annual Commercial Shows at Olympia. Suddenly fixed roofs and more comfortable seats were being offered. But all this was put on hold with the start of the First World War in 1914 – right through to the Armistice in 1918.

With the arrival of the internal combustion engine at the turn of the century, it was inevitable that it would mean the eventual demise of the horse-drawn 'charas'. The speed of this demise is clearly demonstrated by the events that were happening among the hackney Carriages in London. In 1903 there were over 11,000 horse-drawn hackneys on the streets of London, 7,449 hansom cabs and 3,905 'growlers' – those who carried the heavy luggage. But within the next decade, leading up to the First World War, the number of hansom cabs had fallen to 386 with just 1,547 'growlers' remaining. Despite the hansom cab being the most popular hackney ever used by the taxi trade, they were beautifully balanced and could reach speeds of 17 mph – today's average speed in London is estimated at just 11 mph! And, despite Prime Minister Disraeli theatrically describing them as, 'the gondolas of London', their days were numbered, and now these beautifully designed vehicles were being broken up for firewood and sold at one shilling per bag!

Some thirty-eight different companies had sprung up to manufacture taxis leading up to the First World War because they were so profitable. But the then Home Secretary, one Winston Churchill, flatly refused any fare increases for taxis until after the Armistice in 1918 – some eighteen years with no increase. Consequently, the vast majority of these manufacturers went broke and, by the outbreak of the First World War, just one make of taxi was plying for hire on the streets of London, the old and worn-out Unic.

Incidentally, the word 'hackney' has nothing whatsoever to do with the East London borough of that name. It is a derivation of the Flemish term *'haquene'* – a dappled grey horse which originally came from Flanders!

'Charas' After the First World War

During the First World War, the manufacture of charabancs ground to a halt because the military required all the existing chassis – and more. In fact, by the time the war had ended, many thousands of chassis had been supplied by all the major manufacturers. Dennis Brothers of Guildford, Surrey had supplied a massive 7,000 chassis during the war, Leyland Motors 6,000 and Albion Automotive of Scotstoun, Glasgow, some 5,000 chassis. Albion Motors, as it was later named, had a long history of building heavy chassis and was well known for its catchy slogan, 'As Sure as the Sunrise'. For ten years from 1909 they had been famous for manufacturing strong, reliable trucks, before switching to charabanc construction after the First World War. They were eventually swallowed up by Leyland Motors in 1951.

Consequently, when war ended the military had a massive surplus of chassis that weren't required, so they started selling them back to their original suppliers at knock-down prices. These were quickly converted into charabancs and sold on to willing companies.

Thus began the restart of the long love affair between the British working classes and the charabanc, which was to last right through the 1920s – before the popularity and convenience of train travel finally killed the love affair. But the charabanc still retained its popularity among the masses for a day out at the seaside, because you couldn't possibly get the same camaraderie in an old train carriage that only seated half a dozen people – could you?

But progress always brings changes and, as the British economy started to pick up in the fifties and sixties, so the poorly paid mill workers suddenly found that they were getting more wages. Coupled with that, the government were busy introducing a new law requiring mill owners to give their workers a week's paid holiday once a year. So was born the well-known Northern holiday break of 'Wake's Week', when everything shut down. For sure many mill workers still headed for their favourite seaside towns like Scarborough, or Blackpool – or even a whole week at the new holiday camps springing up around Skegness. But now it wasn't just the old man going off with his mates for a boozy day out. Now it was *all* the family with the kids in tow – and in the comfort of a train, or even in their very own car! No more bumpy old 'charas' anymore, they were now a thing of the past!

Opposite above: Jacket cover showing Elizabeth the steam chara blowing her tanks in Whitby Bay, Yorkshire.

Opposite below: A classy modern Volvo Van Hool WSP.

This page: The good folk of Wirksworth, Derby, enjoying a day out in their open-topped charas – *c.* 1895.

Charlotte, the 1929 Dennis chara, lovingly restored by Vernon Smith to continue her popular trips around Whitby Bay, Yorks.

Inset: The early covered-top chara in Wirksworth in the early twenties.

A grand old 1939 Bristol.

Another ancient old girl. No power steering or automatic gearbox with this one. You needed to double the clutch every time you changed gear!

2

GREY-GREEN COACHES AND ME, THE 'CHARA' DRIVER

The history of Grey-Green Coaches has always held a particular interest with me because, in the late fifties, I became one of their 'chara' drivers – but by that time we had the more up-market name of 'coach driver'. Another link that I find fascinating is the fact that my son's best mate from his school days, some forty years ago, is called Dominic Ewer and he is the great-great-grandson of the founder George Ewer!

There is an interesting story worth telling about my entry into the world of the 'chara' drivers. I had already signed on to do the Knowledge of London exams to become a London cabbie, I was out of work, and I needed a decent part-time job that would enable me to complete the arduous task of learning many hundreds of 'runs' and many thousands of 'points'. The thought of driving a 'chara' in the busy summer weekends would suit me just fine, but you needed a PSV licence (Public Service Vehicle licence) to drive one. So, after you had booked your PSV driving test, you needed to hire a 'chara' for the day – and pay for the privilege out of your own pocket. So, I duly booked the driving test and made arrangements to hire a 'chara' on that day from Empress Coaches of Bethnal Green in London's East End. The test went very well because I already had a licence to drive heavy goods vehicles (HGV), and the little Welsh examiner said at the end, 'You're a bit heavy on the clutch, but you'll do boy-o.' Strange to relate, but a year later after I had completed the Knowledge, the very same little Welsh examiner took me out in the taxi for my driving test. Halfway around the course he said to me, 'I think I've seen you before boy-o, have you failed before?' After I informed him, with a big smile on my face, that he had passed me the previous year to drive a forty-nine-seater 'chara', he knew that I knew he couldn't possibly fail me in a four-seater taxi!

Grey-Green Coaches can trace its origins back to 1885, when George Ewer started the business with a horse bus in Stamford Hill and, with the advent of the internal combustion engine, he shrewdly realised that this was the way forward for his business. Like many other coach operators at the time, in order to utilise his vehicles for the whole year, he had two different bodies for each vehicle, a 'chara' body for the summer and a truck body for the winter. His business started to flourish, with many summer day trips in his 'charas' to all the South Coast resorts and a steady turnover for his haulage business in the winter.

His son Henry, who had taken over when his dad retired, carried on building up the business with various takeovers. When he eventually retired, he left it to his three sons to sort out the business, but after a massive bust-up among the boys, another Henry took over the helm and his brothers went their own different ways. Henry number two was one of the first to realise the vital importance of securing regular service routes that would operate all the year round. With these in his hands he could concentrate fully on his lucrative coach business. His first service route – and still running successfully to the present day – was London to Ipswich in June 1928. I drove this service route many dozens of times at night in the late fifties as a punishment for leaving a mental patient stranded at Colchester. Mind you, nobody had bothered to tell me about this mental patient, but I became the sacrificial lamb to protect the company's reputation. This night run – that none of the drivers wanted – was nicknamed 'the Ghost Train' and entailed leaving the old Kings Cross Coach Station at 10 p.m. and 'sweeping up' any late passengers at all the service stops to Ipswich, then on to Felixstowe. You then had to drive back to the Ipswich garage that we shared with the local cabbies and try and get a few hours' sleep on the back seat with a blanket and pillow. The cabbies would wake you up about 5.30 a.m. with a cup of tea, ready to head back to London on the service route at one minute to six! One of the old-timers in our garage informed me that there was a good short-cut from Felixstowe to Ipswich via Manningtree, but to make sure the sun roof was closed when going under the low railway bridge. One dark night I remembered his advice and decided to use his short cut. But hey, I was tired and weary and as I went under the low bridge I heard the tinkle of breaking glass and part of the sun roof was ripped off. I dumped the coach back at the garage the next day without telling anyone about the incident, but the coach was soon traced back to me and, once again I was in trouble with Henry the boss-man, who didn't take any prisoners! In fact what Henry said was 'the Bible' at Stamford Hill – he wouldn't even allow any unions in his premises and any agitators were soon given the sack! I duly appeared before the boss-man and admitted my guilt. This time around my punishment wasn't too bad – except that it hindered going out on my scooter to do my 'runs'. I was to pick up the 'boss-man' most days and drive him up to the Colchester office in his brand-new

Jaguar! Sometimes, I even left him there overnight and literally bombed it back to London in his 'Jag'!

After completing my penance as a chauffeur, my being lumbered with 'the Ghost Train' as an ongoing punishment suited me fine. It gave the time off in the day to do the Knowledge even though I was absolutely knackered by mid-afternoon. So, much to the amazement of my fellow drivers, I volunteered to do it on a permanent basis. Off I would go in the dead of night with all my 'runs' pinned on to the dashboard – so I could learn by reciting them. One night, when we were bombing along in the heart of Essex, a nice guy came up to me and asked if I had a problem because he could hear me mumbling away to myself. We had a good laugh when I explained what I was doing and, he even helped by calling over my precious runs for me to recite!

I did manage to get day trips to the seaside at some summer weekends when it was madly busy in the garage, but for the rest of the year the best jobs that paid out good 'beer money', like a day out at the races, always seemed to go to the same faces! As for us 'second-class' drivers, we were handed the school runs – obviously no 'beer money' there – or the 'change-overs', which entailed driving a full coach-load of people up to Colchester and changing over with a driver who had also brought a full coach load from Great Yarmouth. Then both drivers returned to where they had first started their day – again, no 'beer money'! I had a lot to learn – like giving the foreman a 'back-hander' before he dished out the jobs, the same unfair system they used down the docks for many years. My very first day trip – still with no 'beer money', was to Dunstable Zoo and I was handed the oldest 'chara' in the garage, come to that, it could well have been the oldest 'chara' in London! I think it was an ancient Leyland, but the other drivers had nicknamed it 'the Conker-Box' because it shuddered like mad when ticking over. The driver was isolated in a little box in the front and you even had to double-de-clutch to change gear!

I thoroughly enjoyed the days out with the day trippers, mostly employees from many of the East End factories, and who were very generous with their 'beer money' at the end of the day – especially if, like me, you could tell a good joke and give a song on the mic in the pub. One of the silly pranks that we drivers got involved with – especially with a boozy pub outing, was what we called 'the Lottery Wheel'. The driver would first do a head count that might add up to say thirty punters. He would then collect 'a tanner' off each of them – that equates to about two and a half pence in modern coinage – and each punter was given a number from one to thirty. The driver would then go to the nearside rear wheel of the 'chara' and, with a piece of white chalk, print thirty numbers all around the edge of the tyre. The final piece in this game – with all the punters watching, was to put a chalk mark on the body directly above the wheel. When the 'chara' stopped at its seaside destination, all the punters would clamber out and rush back to discover the winner. It was quite simple, the punter with the number directly under the chalk mark on the body was the winner of over one pound! If the wheel happened to stop between two numbers at equal distance, those two numbers would share the prize! All bets were cancelled if the heavy rain washed away the chalk marks. One of the driver's perks with this soppy game was if it was repeated on the way home, then invariably the driver would cop the winnings from the now boozy punter as his 'beer money'!

But there were strict, unwritten guidelines that you as a driver had to adhere to – especially with a party of all ladies. For sure they were all swigging the beer in the back and having a great time, but God help any young driver who fancied taking a liberty with one of the ladies. I heard a story of one such young driver who was promptly de-bagged, then had his private parts tarred and feathered! It always made me laugh when, after about an hour on the road in a 'chara' with no toilet facilities, the lovely East End ladies would all start singing the same chorus in unison, 'We are dying for a wee-wee, we are dying for a wee-wee.' That was the signal to pull over to the nearest grass verge and let the ladies out. Again, it was the same unwritten guidelines that applied – the driver remained in his seat while all the ladies squatted behind the hedgerow. Eventually all the large pubs with car parks that sprung up along the popular seaside routes – commonly known as 'halfway houses' – realised that 'charas' could mean big business. Mind you, it took them some time to get their toilet facilities right. Can you possibly imagine some 150 people or more from half a dozen 'charas', all queuing patiently to use just *one* male toilet and just *one* female toilet?

The camaraderie that sprung up during the day with passengers and their drivers improved the 'beer money' no end – in fact some of the event organisers actually asked for me by name! I thoroughly enjoyed my year as a 'chara' driver, but after having been a London cabbie for nearly half a century, the diesel is now deep in my veins!

But back to the Grey-Green service routes. The securing of the London to Ipswich route was quickly followed in the early thirties by the London to Harwich service route. The shrewd and clever Henry Ewer was keen to capture the whole of the East Anglian service routes, so later in the thirties he made several important takeovers. First up was Eva's Coaches with a fleet of forty-five, then Sid Page Ltd (Bee Line), and W. H. Jacobs (Monty's Super Coaches); the last two covered East Anglia. Then there followed takeovers of the routes formerly run by the Prince Omnibus Company of Edmonton and Eclipse Motor Coaches.

When the Second World War arrived everything stopped for around six years, when many of the 'charas' were adapted as personnel carriers. But, in 1945, Henry continued with his takeovers. First up was the Baker Brothers Fleet, then in 1952 it was Fallowfield and Britten of Hackney and Ardley Brothers Ltd. Later in the fifties Grey-Green managed to capture its biggest prize so far, Orange Luxury Coaches of

Brixton. All the Orange coaches bore the royal crest because they were the official coach makers to the royal family. Then in the mid-fifties Classique Coaches and Black and White Coaches of Walthamstow were acquired. And still the takeovers continued, with the acquisition of the ageing United Service Transport Fleet in 1965 and Birch Brothers Ltd in 1971. This company, which was based near my home in Kentish Town, had a long history stretching way back to when they operated 'pirate' horse-drawn buses in 1847, yet by 1977 their famous red coaches would disappear forever. Henry Ewer adapted a very clever idea to keep his subsidiaries happy – and to keep the bookings coming in from Londoners who had booked with, say, Orange Luxury Coaches for many years. He let them keep their own liveries and their own individuality; in fact, Orange Coaches had the same livery until 1966 and was finally wound up in December 1975. That same year Henry acquired Wimbledon and Mitcham Belle Coaches, Dix Coaches and Universal Cream Coaches. Henry then bought a seventy per cent controlling stake in World Wide Coaches of Camberwell. It continues to run as a separate, high-class touring company running one of the largest Mercedes fleets in the United Kingdom.

Grey-Green evolved into the George Ewer Group of companies, expanding into London bus operations, which became the Cowie Group after the new bus legislation was passed. At one time the group were successfully running twenty service routes in London, including the jewel in their crown, the No. 24 bus route that showed the only green bus livery among the many red buses, all the way through the West End, Whitehall and Parliament Square.

The Cowie Group eventually re-branded itself as Arriva, which is now one of the largest bus groups in the United Kingdom. Not bad after starting with just one horse-bus, is it?

Above and below: Grey-Green coaches in Central London.

Another Grey-Green coach in Central London.

The famous No. 24 Grey-Green double-decker that had a route through all the famous sights in London.

Another old beauty still working in Taunton.

3

LEYLAND MOTORS

Over the many years since the charabanc became popular there have been many well-known manufacturers of charabanc chassis, including Foden, Albion, Guy, Bristol, Commer, Daimler, Dennis and AEC, then lately Volvo. But without doubt the most famous name to be associated with charabanc chassis is Leyland Motors, who eventually took over AEC, their biggest competitor, then were finally taken over themselves by Volvo in 1988, when their famous name disappeared forever.

Leyland Motors first started life in 1892, when James Sumner inherited a small blacksmith and engineering business from his late father. It was based in Leyland, a small town near Preston in Lancashire. James loved to fiddle with newfangled ideas – especially his passion for steam – and when a neighbour gave him an old lawnmower, he attached his prototype steam engine to it and it was an instant success, winning him the gold medal at The Lancashire Agriculture Show. So he started making these steam lawnmowers and flogging them for £85 each – an awful lot of money in those days – but James reckoned shrewdly that if his customers were wealthy enough to have their own lawn, then they would readily pay the going rate!

The company expanded after extra finance from a new partner, and James decided that steam was the traction for the future, so he designed a steam bus to carry passengers. This was successfully launched in May 1899, with a top speed of just 8 mph and a capacity to carry eighteen passengers. It was promptly sold to the Dundee Bus Company. His company then moved to larger premises and changed its name to the Lancashire Steam Motor Co., and it was soon producing some twenty steam buses every year with its extended workforce. As a point of interest, the last remaining working steam bus in the United Kingdom still plies her trade in Whitby, Yorkshire. The Whitby Steam Bus & Charabanc Co. Ltd is run by Vernon Smith and his family, and their steam bus is lovingly called Elizabeth – but more about the Smith family in a later chapter.

James started fiddling with his idea of creating an internal combustion engine that he believed – quite rightly – would be the future of transport, and in 1904 the company tried out their first petrol-driven vehicle nicknamed 'the Pig'. This was shown at the Olympia Exhibition in 1907, with the petrol-driven engine getting very good reviews in all the motoring magazines. Finally in 1907 the company changed its name again to Leyland Motors Ltd.

Business was booming with Leyland Motors, and they moved into bigger premises with a workforce of around 150. His factory producing steam traction was moved to smaller premises in Chorley, because the work was diminishing. Then in 1912, with the possibility of war on the horizon, production was slowly grinding to a halt. But they were saved when the War Office cut a deal with them should war break out. It was agreed by both parties that Leyland would supply the government with all their heavy lorry chassis immediately at the current market price – plus 25 per cent in the event of war. When it appeared that war looked inevitable the government purchased a massive eighty-eight heavy chassis, which boosted Leyland's coffers and got them out of trouble. Then in 1915 the RAF ordered a staggering 6,000 chassis from Leyland's, because by that time it had been proven that their heavy chassis were the most suitable for military work.

When war finally ended, Leyland Motors discovered that many of their RAF chassis were appearing cheaply on the market, so to save their reputation, in 1919 they purchased a former munitions factory in Kingston-on-Thames and re-bought some 3,000 chassis from the RAF – at a very favourable price of course. These they carefully reconditioned to strict company specifications and sold them on.

The 1927 Commercial Motor Show saw the unveiling of Leyland's brand-new charabanc, the Tiger, and every model since has been named after an animal. In the same show a few years later they displayed their very first diesel engine and their next charabanc model, the Lion, quickly followed by the Lioness. This was followed in 1931 by the Terrier, then the Hippo in 1934, the Badger in 1935 and finally the Lynx in 1938, just before the outbreak of the Second World War.

During the war years all production was directed at manufacturing all sorts of military chassis, and production for the private market only stuttered to a start in the early fifties, with the arrival of their Royal Tiger. This was followed by the Leyland Tiger Cub in 1952 – incidentally my favourite drive from my coaching days. In 1954 they introduced the Leopard, which was so popular it was on the market until 1982. The Tiger was re-introduced in 1981; this was a far cry from the early Tigers, and this Royal Tiger Doyen production lasted until 1993.

Leyland, with its long and illustrious career, was eventually merged into the British Motor Corporation and in 1988 came its death-knell, when Volvo took over the company. Volvo even cancelled the manufacture of the popular Royal Tiger Doyen – possibly thinking it might affect their sales – and they never used the name Leyland ever again!

An old Leyland Tiger.

Above: Another Tiger, not so old.

Opposite above: A Leyland National.

Opposite below: A large Leyland Weyman.

Above: A monster Olympian.

Opposite above: An old Panther Cub.

Opposite below: A seaside trip in a Leyland Atlantean.

Above: A Leyland Leopard.

Opposite above: A smart Leopard.

Opposite below: A brightly liveried Optare Versas.

Another Leopard.

4

THE 'CHARA' STILL RETAINS ITS POPULARITY

Even though the mass popularity of the charabanc has long gone, with even the lovely old name being replaced by the boring word 'coach', there are many companies in rural areas all over the United Kingdom that continue to make a good living from their charabanc trips. I suppose one of the most popular and famous of all the charabanc operators – thanks to their involvement in TV shows and the Harry Potter films – is the Whitby Steam Bus & Charabanc Co. Ltd, run solely by the Smith family. Dad Vernon is the master and chief repairer of this grand old lady, and his monthly blog, highlighting all her many 'illnesses', makes for a good read!

I must confess that as a cynical old cockney, even I am taken with the story that surrounds the long history of their two vehicles. Their lovely old steam bus/charabanc Elizabeth dates from 1931, when it was built in the Sentinel Waggon Works in Shrewsbury. It is listed as a DG6P, a double-geared six-wheeler with the brand-new pneumatic tyres. From 1931 until the late 40s, she toiled for the Cement Marketing Company, then as a tar sprayer in the north-east; her new owners were the well-known road contractors Glossops. Here she ended her first working life, before passing through the hands of many enthusiastic owners for the next forty years, before being snapped up by Vernon Smith in 2002. He toiled on the loving restoration project for many years before vigorously lobbying the Secretary of State to change the Road Traffic Act to allow Elizabeth to carry passengers. Amazingly, this was finally agreed and she was ready for another life! Elizabeth is the only working steam bus/charabanc in the country that is allowed to carry passengers!

The Smiths' other old beauty, Charlotte the charabanc, is even older. She was built in 1929 by Dennis Brothers of Guildford and started life as bus No. 4 in Llandudno, Wales, and from the summer of 1930, right up to the end of 1955, she had the gruelling task of giving tours around the Great Orme. This she did admirably before retiring some fifty-six years ago. Then step forward one Mr Hayes of Luton, who purchased her, with Charlotte having to endure some amazing journeys. She criss-crossed all over Europe, crossing the Alps and climbing up the Vesuvius Pass, all this while towing a matching trailer full to the brim with the hardy passengers' luggage! In 1971, she gave regular trips to Amsterdam!

By some quirk of fate she was found deteriorating in a northern barn by a friend of Vernon Smith and the full restoration began, taking many years before she was brought back to her full beauty. When complete, she obtained her all-important status as a passenger-carrying vehicle. I really must pay a visit to Whitby soon because these stories fascinate me, and Vernon's tours around Whitby in that grand old steam bus seem like my cup of tea – especially now I've seen her on TV making a guest appearance in the Lord Mayor's Show. It appears that Vernon and his missus drove the old lady all the way down to London from Whitby – a total of twelve days – because the old lady doesn't travel very fast. Apparently it will take them another twelve days to get home – that's either complete dedication or superb marketing!

Many other towns and villages across the country have purchased an old 'chara' and continue to run popular tours of their well-known landmarks. In fact, it would appear that their businesses are flourishing because the public's perception seems to have turned full circle. Where it was once all the rage to pack the kids in the back of the family car and spend a day in the country; now, with the spiralling cost of fuel, the ever-increasing traffic congestion and the lack of parking facilities, it's so much simpler to let the 'chara' take the strain!

Another popular adaptation of the 'chara' has been taken by the travellers, who now use them extensively as mobile homes. No more gaily-painted gypsy carts pulled by an old nag, not a bit of it, these modern travellers have moved up-market and gone for the spacious old 'charas'. The Travellers Web Site is well worth a look if you're interested in old 'charas', there are literally hundreds of pictures of them from all over the world. It would appear that the modern traveller is just not content to roam around the United Kingdom because now, with the aid of their 'charas', they can roam around Europe – and even farther afield.

All the girls and boys line up in front of the chara in Caledonian Road, ready for a boozy day out in Southend. The author, with the cropped hair, is in the back row in the centre, *c.* 1952.

A quaint old English Duple parked in the shadow of a German giant with all mod cons, including toilets and up-to-date reclining seats.

This and next page: Elizabeth being prepared for her tours around Whitby Bay.

Above: A 1941 Bristol still doing tours.

Opposite above: Vernon cranks up Charlotte.

Opposite below: A lick of paint and a service and this old girl is ready to go to work.

Above: They don't come much older than this 1949 Bristol.

Opposite above: You can't beat a tour of the seafront!

Opposite below: An old Bedford Duple.

It's worth a ride in this Bristol – just for the colour!

A trip around lovely Bournemouth – why not? The sign says it all – right back to 1969.

Above: Where on earth are Widecombe and Becky Falls?

Opposite above: A Leyland National.

Opposite below: A Bristol Western National heading for Bristol.

Another Bristol bound for Bristol.

But this Bristol is staying in town.

This Bristol is bound for Aberdare in Wales.

5

SOME OF THE CHARABANC LEGENDS FROM THE PAST

Looking through the UK list over the past century of all the wonderful old charabanc companies that successfully plied their trade, it's sad to think that these household names are no more. Due to privatisation – followed closely by nationalisation – these individual founders, who in many cases had worked their fingers to the bone back in the late twentieth century to get their tatty old businesses up and running, must be turning in their graves!

First up way back in 1880 was Thomas Elliott of Bournemouth, who set up his business of horse-drawn vehicles for hire in Branksome Mews – as well as providing coach building, saddlery and blacksmithing. He named his first company as 'Royal Blue and Branksome Mews', and after his first four-in-hand stagecoach service from Bournemouth to link up with the railway at Holmsley was made redundant, after the railway extended the line to Bournemouth, he turned his attention to charabancs. In 1888 his Royal Blue 'charas' on their day trips became a familiar sight around Bournemouth and the New Forest.

Sadly, Thomas died in 1911 and his two brothers took over the business. They introduced the first motor charabanc to their fleet in 1913 and motors quickly replaced horses. During the rail strike of 1919, they started the Bournemouth express service to London. This proved so popular and successful they duly increased the service to twice a week the following year – then twice daily in 1921. By 1926 'Royal Blue' was operating some seventy-two 'charas' – or 'Express Coaches', as they were now called. In 1928 'Royal Blue' obtained licences to operate their services to other cities: Birmingham, Bristol and Plymouth, and by 1930 they were operating eleven routes.

The Road Traffic Act of 1930, to regulate competition for passenger road transport, led coach operators to either eliminate the competition by buying them out, or share services and pool revenues within the consortium. 'Royal Blue' in fact became one of the founder members of Associated Motorways, which coordinated the routes of six major coach operators. But come the end of 1934, 'Royal Blue' was sold to the Tilling Group.

In 1947 the Tilling Group sold its bus operations to the British Transport Commission, which was government-controlled, but the fuel shortage crisis, which deterred drivers undertaking long distance journeys, was good news for the express coaches and business started booming. Then came the Beeching railway cuts in the early sixties, which generated more customers for 'Royal Blue', and in 1965 traffic peaked to a record 1.5 million passenger journeys.

The famous 'Royal Blue' name was shunted from one government-owned company to another. First it was the National Bus Company in 1969, then National Travel in 1972, which eventually became National Express. In 1986 National Express decided to drop all regional names, so after a glorious 106 years, the famous 'Royal Blues' were no more!

While we're talking about Bournemouth, it is worth mentioning 'Yellow Buses' of Bournemouth with its bright-yellow buses – many of them Dennis Dart coaches – and its slogan, 'The Brighter Bus Company'. The company's origins stretched back to 1902 when Bournemouth Council began operating trams, and in 1906 they introduced bus services to act as feeders to the tram system. In 1933 more bus services were started away from the tram system, and eventually trolley buses replaced the trams in 1936. Come the late sixties, diesel buses replaced the 'trollies'.

The Transport Act of 1985, which deregulated and privatised bus services, left the Conservative Bournemouth Council with a problem. They didn't want to lose their popular and lucrative bus service, so they formed a private company and called it 'Yellow Buses Bournemouth' and managed to retain it as a commercial company. But they were replaced soon afterwards by the Liberal Democrats, who decided that because of the ever-increasing financial pressures in 2005, plus the fact that the ageing fleet needed modernising, they would sell it off.

So after 100 years of successful municipal operations, 'Yellow Buses Bournemouth' was sold to Transdev, with the council retaining a 10 per cent shareholding. Transdev set about giving the network a complete overhaul and renewed most of the fleet. Transdev is arguably one of the most successful bus operators in England, with a patronage growth of 40 per cent since 2005 and currently carrying 13 million passengers every year. Yet by March 2011 they sold the company to the giant French government-owned RATP Group. RATP basically run most of the transport systems in Paris – including the Metro, the bus system and most of the tram services. It also owns some twenty-seven transport services worldwide, including the Metrolink Light Railway System in Manchester, as well as the famous 'Yellow Buses of Bournemouth'. I can't get my head around this selling off of England's heritage to foreign governments!

Next up is the once all-powerful Tilling Group, one of the two huge groups – with British Electric Traction (BET) – who controlled almost all of the major bus operations in the country between the wars – until nationalised in 1948. In my boyhood days as a London cockney during the Second World War, Tilling Coaches were so famous that the name was included in the famous cockney rhyming slang as, 'my Dad gives me a Thomas Tilling a week pocket money'. That means of course 'a shilling'!

Yet Thomas Tilling, born in Hendon, Middlesex in 1825, started his one-horse bus business in Peckham, South London in 1846 from very humble beginnings. In fact the story goes that he had to borrow £30 from a friend to buy the old horse! But that thirty quid was well spent, because by 1850 he had obtained permission to run a horse bus service from Peckham to Oxford Street. By sheer hard work and dedication, come 1856 he had a total of seventy horses! These were loaned out to various small businesses on a daily or weekly basis – maybe even to my fellow cabbies of the day! Thomas Tilling was either very clever or very lucky, because ten years down the line in 1866, the Metropolitan Fire Brigade was formed and they badly needed someone to train and supply horses to pull the fire tenders. Thomas was their man; in fact by the time of his death in 1893, he owned a staggering 4,000 horses!

His two sons Richard and Edward – along with son-in-law Walter Wolsey, took over the running of the business and in 1897 they changed the company name to Thomas Tilling Ltd. The company was doing very well, so much so that by 1905 they were operating twenty motor buses, with a massive 7,000 horses for their 250 horse buses. In 1907 they opened the first bus route to outside London with their service from Oxford Circus to Sidcup in Kent. Richard died in 1929, and just two years later in 1931, the family association with the company finally ended. The company, now under new ownership, continued to gobble up their weaker opposition. Their biggest prize to date came in 1935 when they took took over the well-known Royal Blues of Bournemouth. This was a major acquisition because the Royal Bournemouth Blues were the premier coach service in the South and West of England.

The arrival of the Second World War more or less put paid to any coach business, with many of their vehicles being requisitioned for military activities. Then in 1947 came the Transport Act that basically nationalised all the coach companies. In 1968 the National Bus Company was formed, mainly from Tilling and BET subsidiaries. But even today people still call them 'Tilling Reds' or 'Greens'.

Both George Ewer's Grey-Green business and Leyland Motors started up in 1895, as did Dennis Brothers of Guildford, Surrey. John and Raymond Dennis made bicycles and sold them from their Guildford shop. Over the years the business prospered, and they started making motor cars from their new factory in town. After the First World War they switched to making charabancs, buses and many other such large vehicles. Their most famous legacy, and still working in many areas of the country, was the Dennis fire engine.

Next up was the famous 'Midland Red' that evolved in Birmingham in the early 1900s and was acquired by British Electric Traction (BET) in 1905. But their name lived on right through until 1981. 'Midland Red' was the trading name of Birmingham and Midland Motor Omnibus Company (BMMO), one of the largest English bus operators and another founder member in 1934 of the AMC (Associated Motorways Consortium). In 1921 they started express coach services to far-off places like Weston-Super-Mare and Llandudno, as well as their regular routes in Birmingham.

With the arrival of the M1 and the ever-expanding motorway network in 1959, 'Midland Red' started to order more powerful coaches to begin their non-stop express services from Birmingham to London, then later, Coventry to London. After the completion of the M5, they started a non-stop service to Worcester from Birmingham.

From 1977 onwards the company re-branded itself into local area names and each new network spawned a localised brand. In 1981 'Midland Red' was split into six new companies and renamed 'Midland Red Coaches'. Today the old company is no more, after their service routes were all taken over by the conglomerates Arriva, First and Stagecoach.

Next up is the Southdown Coach Company founded in 1915, who really did rule the waves in southern England for many years. Most every route from the South Coast to London was covered by Southdown and, when the spanking-new Victoria Coach Station was built in 1932, a Southdown coach was the very first vehicle to enter. After the Second World War the company was also the very first to offer a coach trip in Europe, a seventeen-day tour to France and Switzerland. Sadly, like all the other great names, Southdown Coaches lost its fleet name, and its unique livery, when it was swallowed up by Stagecoach in 1989.

Black and White Coaches was the brainchild of George Readings, who ran a coach company in Ewhurst called Surrey Hill Motor Services. But he sold up in 1926 and decided on a change of scenery, so he moved to Cheltenham, where he immediately purchased his first red coach with black-and-white livery. He immediately renamed his growing fleet 'Black and White Coaches' and that name managed to exist until 1976. The business was prospering, with regular local tours and a weekly journey to London, and in 1927 this was extended to three times daily in each direction. Later in the year the service was extended beyond Cheltenham to Tewksbury and Malvern, then extended even further to Worcester

– then Gloucester, Bristol and Hereford. By the end of 1928 the service had reached Ludlow, and George was now operating some twenty-one coaches. But even though Black and White Coaches were successfully operating express services, private hire work and luxury tours, George was starting to feel the pressure of his ever-expanding business. So much to everyone's amazement, on 30 April 1930, he sold the business lock, stock and barrel to BMMO (Midland Red). But the famous brand name managed to survive for another forty-six years.

The Road Traffic Act of 1930 was introduced to try and help coach operators get together and share services, so Associated Motorways was formed to co-ordinate services. In 1934 six coach operators in Associated Motorways decided to pool their services between the Midlands and the South West of England and between London and South Wales. The founder members were Black and White Motor Coaches of Cheltenham, Red and White of Chepstow, Royal Blue, Greyhound – then owned by Bristol Tramways, Midland Red, who owned Black and White, and United Counties of Northampton. The hub for the pool was to be Cheltenham Garage, built by Black and White in 1931. After the Second World War new members joined, Lincolnshire Road Carriages and Eastern Counties in 1956, Crosville in 1965 and finally Southdown in 1972. All the members of the consortium – except Black and White – still continued to operate their own services outside the consortium.

It was absolute mayhem in Cheltenham on a peak summer weekend, with as many as 800 coaches on the road from all over England and Wales and all converging on Cheltenham Garage. Here they would exchange passengers with each other, some going on to Wales and others on their way back heading home to Birmingham or London. People who lived in Cheltenham at that time often talk about a myriad of coaches parked all over town while waiting their turn to get into the garage. I'm told the best show of all was at precisely 2 p.m. on a Sunday afternoon. The garage inspector would stand out in the road consulting his watch, and at a given signal 200 coach engines would roar into life, sending diesel fumes all over the town. Then at his next signal – which was precisely 2 p.m., 200 coaches would all come trundling out *en masse* and start making their way to their various destinations. Then, after the noise and fumes finally died, peace and quiet prevailed in the town.

The Cheltenham Garage was rebuilt on a different site in 1951 with all mod cons, but by the end of the fifties things were starting to change. The M1 motorway was opened in 1959, and as it extended westwards, so the coaches were able to cut their journey times and travel all the way to South Wales without a stopover at Cheltenham. It was a similar picture when the M5 was opened, and the route from Birmingham to Bristol by-passed Cheltenham. Midland Red was manufacturing even bigger coaches with massive engines that could reach speeds of 90 mph and the

Cheltenham Garage was slowly and inexorably becoming surplus to requirements. Only a handful of local coaches were now using the Cheltenham Garage, so when The National Bus Company acquired Black and White Coaches in 1969, the writing was on the wall and in 1973 Associated Motorways was disbanded. In 1974 came the final death-knell for Black and White Coaches; they were acquired by National Transport South West and their famous name disappeared forever. Cheltenham Garage finally closed its doors in 1984 and still remains a pile of debris, with the local council promising to rebuild on the site when the economy picks up!

Above: A white Crosville Volvo Van Hool.

Opposite above and below: Top dogs in the consortium, the famous Royal Blues of the Tilling Group.

The Dennis Dominator.

Another old AEC in good shape.

Another member of the consortium, an old Red and White.

Another major player in the consortium, a Midland Red.

This and next page: A Bournemouth Yellow Bus.

Southdown charas – all snowbound!

A monster Daimler of Bournemouth Yellows.

6

NATIONAL EXPRESS AND THE END OF INDIVIDUALISM

With the various transport acts being pushed through Parliament, it was patently obvious to even the casual observer that the government was hell-bent on nationalising all bus and coach operations. The die was well and truly cast and, following the 1968 Transport Act – and after the government had acquired the Tilling Group and BET, the last of the big private companies – many local bus services were nationalised. Their buses and coaches were marketed as National Express from 1972, but the coach services continued to be operated by the individual coach companies.

The seventies was the heyday of coach travel, with the motorway network drastically reducing travel times and offering a major cost advantage over rail travel. The Transport Act of 1980 saw coaches deregulated and, with the following Act of 1985, buses soon followed.

After the national bus service was privatised, so National Express Holdings Ltd was formed until a management buyout in 1991, with the new company now under the name of National Express Group (NEG). In 1992, after the shares were floated on the Stock Exchange, National Express became a subsidiary company, and by 2001 National Express ended their historic on-board steward/stewardess services, deeming it as 'being old-fashioned and out of date'.

During its early years National Express had virtually no competition whatsoever – even though a number of operators had tried. After deregulation in 1980, the largest remaining of its competitors was the British Coachways Consortium – but by the end of the decade most of them had given up the fight! In 1986, National Express decided to drop all regional names as a re-branding exercise, so after a glorious 106 years, suddenly the famous Royal Blues were no more.

The head office for the National Express Group, which controls most coach and bus services across England, Scotland and Wales – even though most of them are sub-contracted out to local bus and coach companies – is situated above the newly-refurbished Coach Station in Birmingham – the original site of Midland Red's old Coach Station in 1929. It was opened in December 2009 after an extensive refurbishment costing some £15 million, and the famous name given the honour of unveiling the new premises was England football team coach Fabio Capello – what a strange choice!

Victoria Coach Station

After many trials and tribulations Victoria Coach Station finally became the London hub for National Express. But its long eventful history – almost eighty years – is well worth recording.

Way back in 1919 many Londoners – including many ex-servicemen – had the strong desire to visit the seaside and escape the deprivation and the terrible memories caused by the aftermath of the First World War. Many 'chara' companies followed the example set by Turnham & Company, who incidentally had their 'chara' garage in Eccleston Street Victoria – possibly close to the site where the Victoria Coach Station was eventually built. This intrepid company drove their 'chara' to Brighton and advertised their services to a willing public. Many other 'chara' operators copied Turnham & Company and offered day trips to many of the popular seaside resorts. The day trips became a 'must' for the war-weary Londoners, with dozens of fully loaded 'charas' leaving every weekend. This rising popularity was helped even further in September and October of 1919 when there was a railway strike and nothing moved – except 'charas'! Coast-based coach operators provided emergency services to get the stranded rail passengers home. In 1920 many other coach operators decided to get on to this lucrative express business and it required a London-based entity to sort things out.

In April 1925, London Coastal Coaches was incorporated in an effort to solve the problem of all the different coach operators doing their own thing. But with the resulting traffic chaos around Victoria caused by hundreds of parked coaches, it was obvious that a new coach station was required. The 1930 Road Traffic Act was the first indication from the government that they were looking towards making the coach and bus industry more under their control. These two factors led to the building of the Victoria Coach Station in 1932.

Being a street-wise London cabbie for half a century, this imposing building has always fascinated me and, looking down Buckingham Palace Road, it seems out of context with the other, rather sombre Victorian buildings. It was designed by Wallis, Gilbert & Partners in the Art Deco style that was all the fashion at the time, and obviously its grand frontage was pure white.

The coach station services were under the control of London Coastal Coaches, an association of coach operators. This worked fine until the Transport Act of 1947, when the industry went a step closer to nationalisation, and in 1968 it was privatised and renamed the National Bus Company UK (NBC). The NBC was made up mainly of Tilling and BET subsidiaries.

It was in the early seventies when I first experienced the Victoria Coach Station with my young family. I just loved going abroad for my holidays, but this year unfortunately I didn't have much cash. So I scoured all the travel brochures for a 'cheepo' and finally came up with a winner. It was a coach company based in Hertfordshire and it was offering a two-week holiday at a ridiculously low price in Blanes, just south of Barcelona in Spain. I duly paid my money and waited in eager anticipation, but in my excitement I forgot the old adage that says, 'You only get what you pay for!'

We arrived at Victoria Coach Station bright and early with our three little kids in tow and I immediately got a telling-off from my wife by getting on the wrong coach – simply because it said 'Spain' on the front! But finally we were on our way down to Dover and on the ferry to France, then onto the Paris by-pass and down the Autoroute de Soleil. The coach made regular stops because it didn't have any toilet facilities, but by the time darkness fell, I started to feel a bit insecure – especially when the relief driver crashed out in the aisle in his sleeping bag. Because I was an old 'chara' driver I had trouble sleeping, so I gingerly stepped over 'the body', went up and sat next to the driver to keep him company. He wasn't very old and I noticed he was swigging some cough medicine, so naturally I asked him if he had a cold? Not so, apparently the caffeine in the cough medicine helped to keep him awake! There was no such thing as 'elf 'n' safety' in those days!

After what seemed like an age we finally arrived at a small café on the Spanish border that offered just foul-smelling holes in the ground as a toilet facility. But hey, we were finally in Spain and even though I was getting an ear-bashing from my dear wife accusing me of putting the kids at risk, the sun was shining and we must be nearing our destination by now. Then Blanes appeared and after climbing the hill out of town, our home for the next two weeks came into view – a huge camp site! I must confess that in my initial excitement after booking a 'cheepo' holiday, I never read the small print on the contract. But as I said before, 'You only get what you pay for!'

In 1978 London Coastal Coaches was brought back to life and renamed Victoria Coach Station Ltd. In the nineties, major refurbishment work was carried out on the coach station in three stages, with the bill totalling in excess of £5 million, and by 1998 London Transport took over, later Transport for London. The Victoria Coach Station site covers a massive 3.3 acres, with twenty-six coach bays and twenty-one departure gates. It operates 1,200 services to destinations all over the United Kingdom – plus 400 to mainland Europe. Around 10 million passengers pass through its doors every year. The National Express fleet include many foreign-named coaches that are totally alien to me. The Caetano Levante – with vastly improved disabled access. The *Scania Irizar*, Van Hool Alizee, Jonckheere Mistal and Caetano Enigma, Plaxton Elite and The Plaxton Paragon/Panther, the most common type used nationwide.

That's basically the final chapter of the story of the Charabanc after some 150 years. First we had the open-topped horse-drawn 'charas' that gave much joy to the working classes in the twenties. Then the motorised version with two adaptable bodies – later covered to withstand the wet weather. Next up were all the wonderful individually owned 'charas', resplendent in their liveries of many colours. Then 'charas' became coaches, and suddenly the coaches all became a boring white – a bit like clones whizzing around the country! Maybe the coming of privatisation, then nationalisation and the arrival of rail service is progress, but I'm not too sure. I feel as though we have lost part of our national heritage; how can you possible attain any kind of camaraderie in an eighty-seat railway carriage, or on a boring express service coach route? And as for trying to have a sly alcoholic beverage or a friendly sing-song – forget it, because the guard will sling you off the 'rattler' post-haste – as well as calling the 'Ol'Bill' in the meantime!

Call me old fashioned if you will – and I'm often called such. But I still fondly relive the wonderful 'chara' trips I enjoyed in my youth, and my days as a 'chara' driver, and I don't ever want to get 'modern' and become a boring 'white coach man'.

Victoria Coach Station around the Millennium.

Above: A 1939 Bristol.

Opposite above: A Dennis Lancet in the sick bay.

Opposite below: An ancient AEC.

Above: A 1948 Bristol.

Opposite above: A Bristol Royal Blue.

Opposite below: It may be over fifty years old, but it's still in service!

Above: A 1949 Daimler.

Opposite above: A fifties Daimler.

Opposite below: Surely this old girl is not bound for Pennsylvania in the US!

Above: Another old AEC.

Opposite above: A sixties AEC.

Opposite below: A seventies Harrington Grenadier.

Above: This Harrington is bound for Mevagissey.

Opposite above: A British Coachways bound for Scotland.

Opposite below: An AEC called 'King Harry' – I don't believe it!

Above: One of the Grey Cars fleet.

Opposite above: Discover Plymouth in this Leopard!

Opposite below: This Bristol's going to Somerset.

A Volvo going to Sainsbury's?

A charming little Bedford Duple.

A Bristol Greyhound.

This Bristol's bound for Penzance.

Above: A great-looking Volvo.

Opposite above: Another heading for Somerset.

Opposite below: A Western National.

Above: This one's heading for Chester.

Opposite above: A private Devon General.

Opposite below: A very ancient AEC WSM.

Above: The once very popular Black and White.

Opposite above: An Eastern National.

Opposite below: A grand old Leyland Panther Cub.

A Leyland Leopard bound for Matlock.

A Bristol Crosville.

Above: An old Daimler of the Blue Bus service.

Opposite above: A Leyland Leopard.

Opposite below: A Leyland National.

An old Tiger.

An ancient Bedford Beadle.

This and next page: National Express – but still carrying the Black and White livery.

The modern monster – now everything is *white*!